Journey

A tale of a foster youth's journey home

By Carlina Shotwell

This Book is Dedicated to

Foster Youth

CHAPTER ONE

On June 29th a young mother's life changed within a matter of minutes. The thought of her baby boy leaving her womb to enter another woman's life brought tears to her eyes. This young mother knew her baby boy, Peter, would love her as his mother no matter where his life journey would take him.

The time had come for baby Peter to meet his new mother and embark on his new life. The young mother smiled softly as Peter's new mother approached. She leaned over and kissed her precious baby so long and handed him to Ms. Barlow.

Ms. Barlow could only imagine how hard this could be for this young mother to provide her with such a wonderful gift. She was forever grateful. For Ms. Barlow

1

was not able to bear her own seed due to her advancing age.

As the years flew by, Ms. Barlow and young Peter enjoyed many vacations, school performances, and class projects. Ms. Barlow age seemed to be getting the best of her and soon she would need help for even the simplest tasks.

Ms. Barlow reached out to her great friend Mr. Hopkins, the lawyer. She informed Mr. Hopkins of her dilemma and he quickly found a solution for young Peter. As young Peter's belongings became nonexistent in Ms. Barlow's home, Peter began to worry.

"I have always loved you from the day our eyes met Peter." said Ms. Barlow. Peter embraced her; unaware of what Ms. Barlow was trying to say to him. "Remember Mr. Hopkins?" she said as she waved in his direction. Peter just nodded his head yes, as he remained embraced within Ms.

Barlow's arms. "Well Peter, Mr. Hopkins has offered you a great opportunity to meet other children just like you."

She said looking Peter directly in the eyes. "Remember I love you Peter, and I am only doing this because I know it is best." Ms. Barlow said as she kissed his wet cheeks. "Will I see you again?" asked Peter while holding Ms. Barlow hands tightly.

"Of course! At least every Sunday my dear!" Ms. Barlow explained. Young Peter began to dry his eyes and smile for he knew what Sundays had in store.

After saying their last good byes and hugs, Peter and Mr. Hopkins drove away. While Mr. Hopkins proceeded to speak, Peter stared out the back window. Not long after their departure, they arrived to their final destination.

CHAPTER TWO

The house was huge. Wild ivy was growing over the fence. Insects were chirping loudly in the overgrown garden, the gate was wide open and the heat of the summer afternoon was stifling. The children running in the yard did not seem to care about any of that as they laughed and ran about.

Peter did a quick count. The children were ten in number and of different ages from two above — if he was not wrong. He could see a boy and a girl that would be about his own age. There was an older boy that would be around sixteen or so, sitting with a little girl who was obviously the baby of the house.

They were painting in a large book. *They all seem happy,* was Peter's first thought as he took his first step into the gate. The lawyer, Mr. Hopkins had told him that Gran's Yard was the perfect place for him.

He had gone mushy describing what his new home was like, saying Granny Yellow was the most loving soul on earth. *Granny Yellow, what sort of name was that?* Presently, an adult stepped out of the house and all the children stopped playing at once.

He and Mr. Hopkins were now two feet from the porch and Peter froze too. The woman was as small as a mite. She was not even as tall as most of the older children playing in the yard. However, she had a presence that held the children's attention.

Fearfully, Peter looked up at her. This must be Granny Yellow. His eyes traveled from the small feet clad in yellow fuzzy slippers, up the length of jean pants and floral blouse she wore. There was an apron covering the front of the blouse down to her knees. The apron was sunshine yellow.

When he reached her face, he was surprised. If this was Granny Yellow, then someone must have named her wrong. Her eyes were gold, her face was fair and only slightly wrinkled, and she had really yellow hair. She could not be anybody's granny, not even his!

Wonders of all wonders she was smiling at him; Peter! As if to tell him how wrong he was for thinking all that he was, many things seemed to happen all at once. Mr. Hopkins took the remaining two feet that would take him to Granny Yellow and bent over the woman in a hug. "Hello Granny Yellow," he said, enfolding the woman in a bear hug. *"Hello Granny Yellow."* Peter wondered at the name again.

CHAPTER THREE

Peter was still pondering about the children, the woman and the lawyer when suddenly, the children all rushed at the woman and the lawyer. "Uncle Jeremy!" "Uncle Jeremy!" they all called and jumped on his back even as he was still embracing Granny Yellow. It was only then that he remembered that the lawyer had told him to call him Jeremy.

The sight in Gran's Yard was one that Peter had never seen before. He could not forget the smile on the woman's face before the lawyer hugged her; it was sunshine in itself. Suddenly, the children stepped back and stood surrounding the woman and the lawyer.

Peter was now staring at his worn out boots but managed to raise an eye. The children were all staring at him curiously but with smiles on their faces. He quickly snuck a gaze at the woman; there was that sunshiny smile again. He lowered his gaze and stared at his boots again.

"You must be Peter," the woman said. Her voice carried to him strongly and softly at the same time. Peter nodded once. His torn boots were becoming more and more fascinating by the second.

He heard the woman move and he stiffened. Suddenly she was beside him and before he could even breathe, he was in her arms. Just like that, she embraced him dirty boots, faded clothes, unruly hair and all.

"Welcome home Peter," she whispered into his ear softly. He wanted to tell her that he had no home, but he could not. Granny Yellow smelled of butter mint. Peter loved butter mint.

Immediately after the biggest hug that Peter had ever received in his life, Granny Yellow clapped her dainty hands to call the attention of the children. Peter had almost smiled just then, the children were already smiling and watching him and the woman, so there was no need for the clap.

"This is Peter and he is part of the family now," she said to them all. "Yay!" they had all shouted gleefully. His surprise knew no bounds when the children all came to hug him one after the other.

They told him their names with each hug; Michael was the oldest followed by Juliet, Heather, Miguel, Stacy, Irene, Sebastian, Arik, Liam and baby Martha who wanted Peter to carry her. In about two minutes, he had received ten hugs and ten smiles in total. None was as warm as that of Granny Yellow but he did not tell any of them. Afterwards, everything else happened very quickly.

CHAPTER FOUR

Without being told, Michael volunteered to take him inside the house and Stacy grabbed his little, worn out satchel and slung it over her shoulders. Granny Yellow allowed them to bring him inside saying that they should be out in time for snacks. Peter wondered what that meant; it was not even evening yet

. Peter had showered and Michael was still in the room waiting for him. The room was big and beautifully painted with green and white. There were four beds in the room, each with a closet, a bedside drawer, a table filled with books, a chair and a reading lamp. Even with all that, there was still enough room to walk.

He had been told that he would be sharing the room with three other boys. Peter stood at the door of the bathroom wondering what to do next. His clothes were gone. "Heather has come to take your clothes for laundry.

Jimmy said you could borrow his clothes for now," Michael was saying, he was rummaging through one of the closets, "you are about the same size." He came up with a pair of khaki pants and a T-shirt and handed them to Peter. Peter only stared at him in confusion. He had no idea what he was talking about.

Just then, his eyes caught sight of his satchel on one of the beds and he ran to it. He opened it and brought out his favorite pair of pants and another shirt. He quickly put it on, aware of Michael's watchful eyes. When he was done, he hugged his satchel to himself and sat on the bed.

"You don't talk much, do you?" Michael asked. He put the clothes back in the closet and walked up to Peter. Michael sighed heavily and came to sit beside him. Peter scuttled away and sat on the edge of the bed.

11

"You remind me of myself when I came to Gran's Yard nine years ago," Michael said. Peter's gaze flew to the other boy's; *"he had been living here for nine years?"* Michael nodded as if Peter asked the question aloud. "I was scared because I thought it would be like the other homes I lived in," Michael continued with a shake of his blonde hair.

CHAPTER FIVE

Peter stared at the boy in wonder. However, the boy was no longer looking at him; his eyes were far away as if he was remembering. "But when I got here, everything changed," he said. "I was the first kid that Granny Yellow took in when her own last kid went off to college.

I would not let her come near me and I would not leave the bag I came with; I even used it as a pillow. I used to hide under the stairs when she was coming. Nevertheless, Granny Yellow, she made my fears disappear. She gave me new clothes, new shoes and put me in school.

Most of all, she gave me love." Peter was no longer clinging to his bag. He was amazed by the story that Michael was telling him. "I used to think that Granny Yellow would surely change. I mean nobody could be that full of love, especially as she kept taking in more children, but she did not change.

With each child, it seemed the love got bigger. With Granny Yellow, there was always room for more." Michael turned to look at Peter in the eyes. Peter did not remember to duck his eyes. "I will be leaving for college in two years and I can't imagine life away from Gran's yard," he said sadly.

Just then, the door opened and a red head poked in. It was Heather; she was the only red head in the house and would be the same age as Peter. "Michael," she said but she was looking and smiling at Peter, "Granny said it is time for snacks." She waved at Peter and left. Peter liked her smile.

"Okay pal," Michael said and he stood up, "It's time for Granny's afternoon tea and snacks and believe me, you don't want to miss the pie." Michael reached out a hand to help Peter up and Peter stared at it in confusion. He looked up at Michael and saw that he was smiling. "Come on," he said.

That was when Peter knew that he meant to help him up. More than that, he wanted to be friends. He continued to stare at the hand silently. His own hand itched to take the hand but he was scared. He looked into Michael's eyes again and the smile was still there. Gingerly, he reached out a hand and placed it in the outstretched hand. Michael's smile widened and he pulled him up. "Let's go have some pie!" he said.

CHAPTER SIX

They were almost at the door when Michael spoke up again, "There are good foster homes around, when we go visiting other homes you will see," he promised Peter. He must have seen that the boy was having a hard time believing him.

When they reached the dining room, everybody was seated and waiting for them. His eyes immediately sought Granny Yellow. She was seated at the head of the table with Martha on her legs and the lawyer seated to her left.

They were talking and laughing into each other's eyes. Michael took an empty chair and patted the seat beside him. Warily, Peter took the seat. His mouth opened in awe at the feast on the table.

There were sandwiches, muffins, rolls, vegetables and pudding. Peter wondered whose birthday it was.

Throughout the meal, he could feel the happiness in the air. The children chatted and laughed. They talked to him, asking him this and that but he only shook his head or nodded.

They all wanted the woman's attention- "Granny Yellow, please pass the sugar." "Granny I need more pudding." "Granny Yellow, feed me." The woman attended to them all without the least complaint.

Peter knew that he had never seen a person like her. The lawyer too seemed familiar with the children and the woman. Though the jam was right next to Mr. Hopkins, Granny still spread butter on his muffin for him.

Sometimes, he felt her kind eyes on him and when he snuck a look in her direction, she would smile and wink at him. He was charmed by her golden eyes but would quickly look away again.

"Why are you called Granny Yellow?" Peter did not know when he blurted out the question. Suddenly the table went quiet and Peter's heart raced in his chest. They were all staring at him now. *Oh! Why did I go and ask that question?*

CHAPTER SEVEN

Suddenly again, everyone started to talk at once. Each child answered differently. "She has yellow hair!" "She has yellow eyes!" "She likes the color yellow!"

Mr. Hopkins laughed at them all. "Silly children," he said, "Granny Yellow is called so because that is her name." Peter looked at him in confusion. The lawyer smiled at him and said, "She is Mrs. Yellow Hopkins but we all call her Granny Yellow."

Hopkins? Peter gasped in surprise. She was the lawyer's mother. Granny Yellow spoke up. There was a twinkle in her eyes. "I was told that my mother saw my yellow eyes and hair and simply called me Yellow," she said with a smile for him.

Everybody laughed, even though Peter was sure they had all heard the story before. He looked around the table as they laughed, and then looked back at Granny Yellow. Yellow suited Granny Yellow perfectly, she was bright and yellow, just like the sun.

Peter liked the sunshine. He smiled a little. Maybe Michael was right about this place. Gran's Yard was certainly more than he expected. Peter told himself that this time around, he was indeed home.

CHAPTER EIGHT

Without realizing it, hours, days, months, flew by while living with Granny Yellow. Peter was having such a great time making new friends and enjoying his new home.

One morning Peter woke up with a loud yawn and a smile. He looked around the room he shared with the other boys and smiled some more. As usual, he was the first to wake.

Jimmy, Miguel and Ben were all still asleep. It had been four months, one week and five days that he started living with Granny Yellow. Peter smiled again when he remembered the first day he came to Granny Yellow's Yard.

That day, he had not known that he would be smiling this much. That hot summer afternoon, he had no idea that he could ever be this happy. Then of course, he

21

had not known Granny Yellow even though he had heard of her from the lawyer that brought him here. Quickly, he knelt on his bed and said his prayers.

As he had been doing since he learned the blessing of prayers, he prayed first for Granny Yellow. He prayed for all sorts of good things he could think of for her. When he could not think of any more, he simply asked the good Lord to add more by himself.

Afterwards, he prayed for the children in Gran's Yard. They were all so good that surely, the good Lord would want to answer the prayers he said for them.

Granny Yellow had taught him how to pray. Saying his prayers was not the only thing that Granny Yellow taught him to do. He had learned a lot since he stepped his feet onto Gran's Yard.

The first thing Granny Yellow had taught him was that he was home. Of course, he had not believed her.

However, she had continued to teach him every day using all kinds of methods and soon, he had learned Gran's Yard was his home.

Peter also remembered to say a special prayer today for his new best friend Jimmy. It was funny that he was best friends with the last person he had met at Gran's Yard. Peter had counted ten children when he first entered the Yard.

He had no idea that there were four more inside and one other. Jimmy was the one other and Peter loved his best friend very much. He had never had a best friend before and he was glad to have one now.

CHAPTER NINE

When Peter came to live at Granny Yellow's, Jimmy had gone on a weekend visit to his father's. When the boy came back a week later and saw Peter, he had smiled brightly and declared that he liked Peter.

The powerful combination of Granny Yellow and Jimmy soon drew Peter out of his shell. He and Jimmy were now inseparable. Together, they had been up to numerous mischiefs, with more to come.

Finished with his prayers, Peter said 'Amen' and sprung up from the bed. Grinning like a cat, he silently walked barefoot to the bed nearest to him. He silently slid into the bed beside Jimmy.

Silently, he used his pinky finger to tickle Jimmy in his jaw. Jimmy was always a heavy sleeper; he only turned slightly and continued to sleep. "Sleepy head," Peter whispered laughingly. Looking around, Peter beamed happily when he saw a piece of paper on the table next to Jimmy's table.

He picked up the paper, rolled it into a thin piece of cone and used the pointed end to tickle Jimmy's ears. Jimmy slapped at his ear, murmured softly and slept on.

Peter rolled his eyes in frustration. "Wake up Jimmy, it's your birthday!" Peter shouted, giving up on trying wake him so playfully. There was no use waking Jimmy up playfully as he was trying to.

Everybody knew that Jimmy only woke up when he heard loud voices calling. However, Peter had figured that since it was his friend's birthday, he deserved some special treatment.

He should not have bothered; Jimmy was not going to change suddenly just because it was his birthday.

Nonetheless, Peter's scream did the trick just as he knew it would.

Jimmy's eyes flew wide open, the ten-year-old boy stared at Peter for a long second and then he jumped up in bed. "Yay!" he screamed like a warrior, "it is my birthday! Happy birthday to me!"

The two boys began to scream loudly on the bed, holding hands and singing "happy birthday to you/me…" in the loudest voice that they could. Soon, the other boys in the room woke up groggily.

When Miguel and Ben saw the two boys jumping and singing on the bed, the sleep flew right out of their eyes. "Happy birthday Jimmy!" they both screamed. Hurriedly, Miguel and Ben rushed over to Peter and Jimmy. Now, there were four happy boys jumping and singing on the bed. They sang so loudly and laughed so happily that soon, the whole of Gran's Yard was awake.

Chapter Ten

In twos and threes, the children living in Gran's Yard trooped into the boys' room. From the song, they already knew what was happening. They joined in on the song and one by one, they hugged the birthday boy.

When Granny Yellow entered, still in her pajamas, they laughed heartily and rushed to hug her too. "Granny Yellow, it's my birthday!" Jimmy cried happily. Granny Yellow smiled at the silly boys on the bed.

She thought to herself, *The entire neighborhood would know by now with the noise they were making.* "Of course silly, I know it is your birthday," she said with a big smile, "I only wonder how you came to be awake and singing at this time."

They all knew Jimmy. He slept well into the morning if he was not shaken awake. Granny Yellow was right; someone must have woken Jimmy up at this very early time of the day. Peter was already grinning from ear to ear.

Granny Yellow caught his eye and said, "Ah ha! I should have known it would be none other than the early bird Peter!" The children laughed at her words. Since Peter joined them, they named him 'early bird'. Nobody ever woke up before him, not even Granny Yellow. "Well, thanks to your friend here, my six o'clock surprise for you have been ruined," Granny Yellow said slowly with a large, mischievous smile.

"Surprise?" Jimmy asked excitedly. Granny Yellow nodded, there was a twinkle in her golden eyes. Peter was not worried that he had ruined her surprise; he knew that Granny Yellow had her ways. "Why yes," she said, "did you think I forgot about your birthday?" she asked in a teasing voice. The children chuckled at that.

Their Granny Yellow never forgot a child's birthday, even though they were fifteen in number. It never ceased to amaze Peter how she did it. Jimmy flew into Granny Yellow's hands and hugged her fiercely. "Where is it? Where is my surprise?" Jimmy chanted. "You will have your surprise…" Granny Yellow stopped and stared first at the birthday boy and then at the other children.

Every single child in the room was eager to hear about this surprise. Granny Yellow always came up with the most exciting birthday surprises. "… when it is truly morning," she finished at last. "Aww Granny Yellow," they all grumbled. They had been so eager to hear about the surprise. "Off to bed, you all," Granny Yellow said, but with a smile.

CHAPTER ELEVEN

One by one, the children trooped out of the room for their rooms. They all knew when Granny Yellow was serious. Most importantly, they knew that the surprise would be waiting in the morning.

Granny Yellow never made a promise and failed. When Granny Yellow was left with Peter, Jimmy, Miguel and Ben in the room, she went to hug Jimmy one more time. "Happy birthday Jimmy, I love you," she whispered in his ears. "I love you too Granny Yellow," The birthday boy whispered back.

With a wink for him and a smile for the rest of the boys, she left the room. The boys crowded on Jimmy's bed and began to chat quietly. Each began to guess what Jimmy's surprise birthday gift would be. "Maybe it is a trip to Disneyland," Ben said. "No, it can't be," Miguel argued,

"we went there for Stacy's birthday in April, remember?"
The boys nodded.

Granny Yellow never repeated a surprise; she said
every kid was unique and so should have his or her own
unique surprises. Her creativity with surprises never failed
to amaze them all. "Perhaps, she would bake you your
favorite muffins," Miguel suggested.

After arguing back and forth for a while, Miguel
and Ben went back to their beds and slept. Jimmy looked at
Peter lying next to him and they grinned. "Thanks Peter,"
Jimmy whispered. Peter smiled happily, "What are best
friends for?" Together, they stared at the Mickey Mouse
clock that hung on the wall close to the bathroom. They
silently began to count the seconds until morning. It was
4:33 a.m.

CHAPTER TWELVE

If it were his birthday, Peter guessed that he could not be any happier than he was right now. Unknowingly, Granny Yellow had not only given Jimmy the best birthday presents ever, she also had made the day the best for Peter.

Peter knew that he was an orphan and that he was not supposed to wish for too many things. However, Peter tried his best not to, but, he still found himself wishing strongly for one thing. Peter had always wanted to go for a beach picnic.

His wish had come from the time when he was being driven to the Barlow's for the first time. On their way, they had encountered a beach where he saw so many families having a picnic. Peter had so much wanted to join them that he had stared long in the mirror until their car was out of sight.

In addition, today for Jimmy's birthday, the beach was where Granny Yellow brought the entire group of kids from Gran's Yard for the biggest picnic ever. It was as if the woman knew Peter's fondest heart desire and set out to fulfill it.

Of course, Peter knew that there was no way she would know because he never told anyone. In fact, since he got to Gran's Yard, he only thought about his long ago wish a few times. Perhaps, Granny Yellow was an angel. Whatever she was, Peter was immensely happy for the birthday surprise she gave to his best friend and him.

The beach was crowded and teeming with people because it was a weekend. However, they were able to secure a large space for them all. Right now, everyone was having a swell time celebrating Jimmy's birthday.

CHAPTER THIRTEEN

The boys were playing beach ball against the girls while Granny Yellow pretended to be the umpire. Michael, the oldest of them was sitting out with Martha, the youngest of them.

Since Martha could not join in the game, Michael had volunteered to play the baby sitter while they all had fun. Peter found it very odd that three-year-old Martha cheered loudly for the boys while Michael cheered for the girls.

The two were watching the game and fighting over who was going to win. Peter wondered if Martha knew that the girls were leading by one point and the boys were finding it hard to score. Maybe she would support the girls if she knew. However, then again, Martha was so small, she probably liked the colors the boys wore more than what the girls wore.

It was an active friendly match. Nobody was taking winning or losing to heart. They all just wanted to have fun! A small crowd had gathered to watch the match when they were about to start and Peter had almost lost his nerve.

It was the first time Peter would be playing beach ball and he did not want to play in front of an audience... However, when Jimmy led the chant, "Peter, Peter, Peter..." and others chorused it, he pushed his misgivings aside and joined in.

CHAPTER FOURTEEN

Now he was getting the hang of it and thoroughly enjoying himself. He and Jimmy played side by side and Peter could not remember a day when he had been this happy. In fact, since coming to Granny Yellow's, his days had been becoming more and more happy.

With happy thoughts in mind, Peter caught the ball coming from the opposite side and threw it immediately. The girls could not catch it and it was a point for the boys. Everybody hailed Peter for his lucky save, including Granny Yellow.

Peter grinned proudly; the boys and girls now had a draw. Stacy, Heather, Irene, Juliet, Beatrice and Greta playfully stuck out their tongues at Peter and he stuck his at them too. He knew they were only joking and were not the least hurt that the points were now tied.

They continued to play and no side scored another point. Granny Yellow blew the final whistle. The game had ended with a draw and it was all thanks to Peter's last score. The boys rushed over to Peter and carried him on their shoulders. Some patted him on the head; others clapped him on the back.

The girls also smiled at him and told him what a good job he did. They all began to walk back to the shade where food, Michael and Martha awaited them. "I didn't know I could play," he told her truthfully. "Mighty fine play for someone's first time," Granny Yellow said, coming up beside him.

He beamed up at her proudly. The look on her face said she was proud of him; Peter loved making this woman happy and proud of him. Granny Yellow smiled at his surprise at himself. She bent to his eye level and looked him in the eye. "Well, there you have it; if you believe you can and if you believe you can't; you're right," she quoted wisely.

Peter tilted his head in confusion. Granny Yellow sometimes said some confusing words. Though, when he later sat down to think about the words, they made sense to him and they warmed up his heart. This was one of such times. He took a minute to think on it. Granny Yellow smiled encouragingly at him. "Are you saying that whatever we believe of ourselves is the truth?" he asked after a while.

Granny Yellow stood up from her crouch, winked at him and softly whispered, "Bingo!" She ruffled his hair and walked ahead of him. Peter watched as she raced Heather to their stand and wondered for the thousandth time what kind of person Granny Yellow was.

She was an adult who took care of them all; a teenager who played with them all, and a friend who held them all together. When they reached Michael and Martha, both were arguing for their respective team. Granny Yellow broke up the argument with five simple words. "Time to cut the cake," everybody shouted in glee and rushed over.

CHAPTER FIFTEEN

Three weeks prior Peter had thought that theirs was the only foster home with the happiest kids in the world. He was wrong. Before coming to Gran's Yard, he had thought that there were not many foster homes around. He had been wrong then too.

Now, he was seeing with his own eyes other children in another foster home who were having a good life like theirs. They were visiting the Houston's today. Granny Yellow had told them early this Saturday morning that they would be paying the Houston's a visit.

Jimmy had explained to Peter that Nancy Houston was Granny Yellow's friend who also fostered children. She and her husband never had children. Instead, they started taking care of orphans.

On listening to his best friend talk about the Houston's, Peter had looked forward to seeing for himself how the children fared there. Did they have fun like they did at Granny Yellow's? Were they treated well? Were they scared and wished for a better life?

He had a mind to plead with Granny Yellow to take in the Houston kids if they were maltreated. He had worried himself all through the morning and now that they were finally at the Houston's. He saw that he had worried his head for nothing.

CHAPTER SIXTEEN

The Houston's were an elderly couple who were nice and friendly. They had two teenage twin girls who they had adopted since they were babies. The girls were thirteen, well mannered and familiar with Granny Yellow's kids.

When they saw Peter, they wanted to know all about him too. Peter saw that the girls were living well and were happy. They all played together until evening. When it was time to leave, Peter was sorry to go.

He enjoyed being with the Houston's and the girls promised to come to Gran's Yard sometime soon. As they sat in the bus that was taking them back to Gran's Yard, Peter laid his head on the seat rest and observed the sixteen passengers in the bus.

He looked at each child in the bus. His gaze also caught Granny Yellow taking a nap. A few of the kids at Gran's Yard had a single parent and sometimes went home on holidays. Many of them had nowhere to go.

However, Granny Yellow made no separation among them all. She treated them all like her flesh and blood. All of them had one thing in common- they were all happy, single parent or not. Peter knew that they had no one else to thank but the woman sleeping quietly in the front seat in the bus.

Sometimes, she would snap awake and look back to check on the kids seated at the back and then resume her nap. She did that too in the middle of the night. She would go around the house, checking on all the children in their rooms to make sure that they were all fine.

It was on one of her nightly parades that she had noticed Peter quietly crying one night. It was storming outside and Peter was afraid of the storm. Granny Yellow had sat with him held his hands and told him that it was only rain.

To make him believe, she had taken him to the rooftop. Together, they got drenched by the rain. Peter was never afraid of the storm again. Peter turned to his left to check on Jimmy.

His best friend was fast asleep beside him in the bus. Closing his eyes too, Peter happily thought of his day and smiled. They were now heading back home. "Home", Peter thought before he fell asleep, "home sweet home"

Made in the USA
Charleston, SC
30 October 2016